The Martini Book

THE MARTINI BOOK

THE FIRST,
THE LAST,
THE ONLY,
TRUE
COCKTAIL

SALLY ANN BERK

PHOTOGRAPHS BY
ZEVA OELBAUM

BLACK DOG
& LEVENTHAL
PUBLISHERS
NEW YORK

Published by
Black Dog & Leventhal Publishers, Inc.
151 West 19th Street
New York, NY 10011

Distributed by Workman Publishing Company
708 Broadway
New York, NY 10003

Hardcover ISBN: 1–884822–98–3
w v u t s
Paperback ISBN: 1–57912–348–1
j i h g f e d c b
Leather ISBN: 1–57912–188–8
l k j i h g f e d

Acknowledgments

Many thanks to the following people
whose help was invaluable:
Zeva Oelbaum for her beautiful and creative photographs;
Joseph Teresa for his extraordinary food styling;
Karen Berman

Props from the collections of:
Ann Kerman and Bill Boyer
Jonette Jakobson
Steve and Dotty Malinchoc
Peter Malinchoc
Betsy Reid

Dedicated to James, my favorite martini maker

Book design by Jonette Jakobson

Printed in China

CONTENTS

"I know I'm not going to live forever,
and neither are you,
but until my furlough here on earth
is revoked, I should like to elbow aside
the established pieties and raise
my martini glass in salute to the
moral arts of pleasure."

Bob Shacochis
Award-winning novelist and
well-known hedonist

INTRODUCTION

THE MARTINI

The martini is the quintessential American cocktail. Born and bred in the United States, the martini has come to represent everything from sophistication to depravity, elegance to wild abandon. Sometimes called a "silver bullet", it's clean, it's cold, and it always hits the mark.

Presidents and movie stars, journalists and poets, fictional characters and their creators, have all looked to the martini for inspiration, release, love, humor. No other cocktail has such a complicated folklore. No other cocktail engenders the kind of passion true martini purists exhibit when mixing or discussing their unique ways of making a martini.

The origin of the martini has been the subject of much debate. It was discovered sometime during the latter part of the nineteenth century, but beyond that one probable fact, the stories of its origin diverge.

One of five theories places the martini in the San Francisco Bay Area after the Gold Rush. Another places it in Martinez, California, thus the name. Still another theory credits the bartender at the Hoffman House in New York around 1880. A fourth story attributes the martini to an Italian immigrant named Martini di Arma di Taggia, who tended bar at the Knickerbocker Hotel in New York in the early part of the twentieth century. Yet another story has the martini being created in the Netherlands.

There is no doubt that gin was developed in the Netherlands, but not the martini. Too much evidence points to America as its birthplace. New Yorkers usually adhere to the Hoffman House theory, while West Coasters prefer the San Francisco theory.

But why and how did this gin drink become a cultural icon? Why not the Rob Roy? The Rusty Nail? The Manhattan?

All of these drinks have their place among the pantheon of classic cocktails, but the martini captured the fancy and the taste of the people from the moment it was born, and except for a lapse during the 70s, it's remained the quintessential cocktail ever since.

Perhaps its simplicity is what gives the martini its staying power. Perhaps it's the iconic stature of the martini glass. Maybe it's the fact that all you need are the two essential ingredients of cold gin and vermouth to create something sublime. Creating a martini is almost alchemic—from two basic elements, one can create gold or the cocktail equivalent.

Whatever the reasons, the martini is here to stay. Many of us will usher in the next millennium with champagne. Some of us will toast the new age with our silver bullets.

THE
INGREDIENTS

G in or vodka, vermouth, and olives are all that are needed to create classic martinis. Before we look at other flourishes, let's explore these basic building blocks.

Gin comes to us from the Netherlands, where it was called *genievre*, which means "juniper." It is a clear liquor, distilled from grain, and flavored with juniper berries. Popular myth holds that it was first invented as a blood cleanser by a seventeenth century chemist.

Gin's popularity grew throughout Europe and spread to the Colonies. Dickens wrote about gin shops and Hogarth painted them. Henry Hudson brought it with him on his expeditions to the New World. Gin was easy to make because it required no aging. This is why gin became immensely popular during Prohibition, you could distill it anywhere.

There are three kinds of gin available today—Genever, Old Tom, and London Dry. Genever is the original Dutch formula. It is a highly flavored gin and is not usually used in martinis. Old Tom, a non-dry gin, is created when barley malt or sweetener is added to dry gin. It is not readily available, but its cousin, Pimm's Cup, is still served as a cocktail. It is widely believed that the original martini, the Martinez Cocktail, was created with Old Tom gin.

The gin most people know is London Dry. This is the gin served in bars and found in liquor stores the world over. All spirits are distilled once, but the craft of gin-making is exemplified during the second distillation. A gin-smith creates a fine dry gin in the redistillation of the liquor. During this second distillation flavorings are added. It is not unusual to find citrus peels, herbs, and spices added during the second distillation. Without them, a gin martini would not exist.

While one can use almost any kind of vodka to make a good vodka martini, the quality, taste, and smoothness of different gins can make or break the drink. With gin, you get what you pay for, and one should never go for the bargain basement gins. Start with Bombay, Bombay Sapphire, or Beefeater's. Try some others if you like, but keep in mind that because gin is so easy to manufacture, there are many gins that would do better as paint thinners. Since gin is arguably the key ingredient in a martini, it makes no sense to skimp.

The other key ingredient is vermouth. Even though a dry martini uses practically none, it needs to be there. Vermouth is a fortified wine that has been flavored with various herbs and spices. The word "vermouth" comes from the German word *wermut* which means "wormwood." Before wormwood was discovered to be poisonous, it was used in making vermouth (and its notorious relative, absinthe). The martini is made with white dry vermouth,

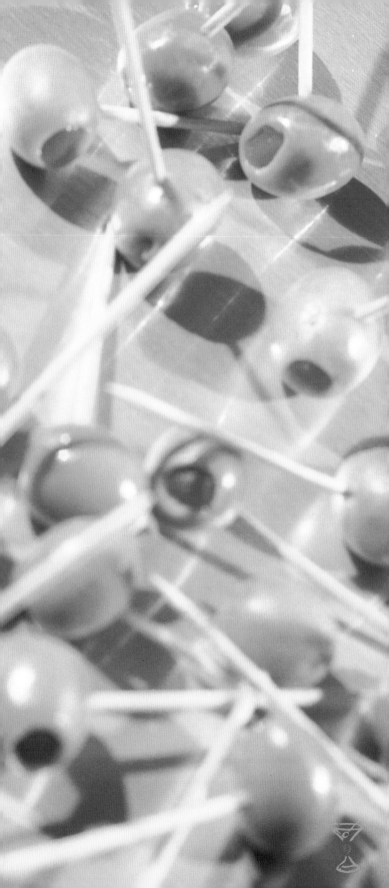

also known as French vermouth, a white liquid that can also be drunk as a cocktail. It should not be confused with bianco, an Italian version, which is also white but much sweeter. Sweet vermouth, or rosso, is a reddish vermouth used in Manhattans. Early recipes for martinis also used sweet vermouth.

Many purists consider the vodka martini a bastardization of a fine drink. Others consider it a legitimate variation and believe it has its rightful place in the martini pantheon. Even though vodka martinis did not become popular until the 1960s, we must consider vodka as an essential ingredient in this new generation of the drink.

Vodka is a Russian word meaning "little water." It has its

origins in Russia, but is made worldwide. It was originally made from distilling potatoes, but can, and is, made from any grain. It is a neutral spirit, which means it must be flavorless by law. It is not aged.

Many people will argue that more expensive vodka tastes better or is smoother. However, vodka shouldn't have a flavor to begin with, unless it is a flavored vodka. The only way to resolve this argument is to buy a bottle of bargain vodka and a bottle of premium vodka, remove the labels, and chill them to freezing. Sip one, then the other, and see if you can tell the difference. You can't. Of course, others will tell you that you can—that Ketel One is better than Stoli, and Absolut is the best. In the end, it's up to you.

What makes vodka interesting is not what's in the bottle, but what's on it. Since the collapse of the Soviet Union, we have access to vodka from such places as Georgia, Kazakhstan, the Ukraine, and other Russian republics. Vodka is also coming to us from Scandinavian countries, other European countries, and Japan. A good liquor store will carry Australian vodka. Absolut vodka has a following based on its advertising campaign, and Stolichnaya is expanding its offerings, selling vodkas flavored with everything from peaches to peppers to coffee. The culture of vodka becomes more intricate every day. We've come a long way since James Bond sipped his Smirnoff.

The quintessential garnish for a martini is an olive. Olives are a bitter fruit that originated in the Mediterranean. They require a multistep curing process to become edible. First they are soaked in an alkaline solution, then fermented in brine or salt to reduce bitterness and tenderize the flesh. After curing, some olives marinate in vinegars or herb mixtures to give them signature taste characteristics. They vary in color from an unripe pale green through pinkish-brown to fully ripened jet black, and come in a wide range of sizes and shapes. Ancient trees growing in the rocky soil of Italy, Spain, Greece, and Israel still bear fruit. Olive production is big business in California as well.

The most common olive used to garnish a martini is the Spanish olive. It is a small green olive, sometimes stuffed with a pimento. (The less commonly used black olive makes it a Buckeye Martini.)

Many different kinds of olives are widely available in delis, gourmet stores, and even supermarkets. To learn about olives and what you like, the best thing to do is taste them. You can invent your own variations on the martini by using different olives. Some dry martini aficionados like to replace the olive brine in a jar with vermouth. These vermouth-soaked olives make great garnishes for martinis, and make it unnecessary to use any vermouth in your drink.

SETTING UP YOUR MARTINI BAR

I t is easy to set up your own martini bar in your home or office. You will need the ingredients (discussed in the previous section), of course, and certain equipment. This book contains recipes that go far beyond the basic martini. In order to make all the drinks in this book, and create some of your own, you will need more than vodka or gin, vermouth, and olives.

Be sure to have at least eight martini, or cocktail, glasses. These triangle-shaped glasses are the symbol of the drink. They are made of glass and can be found in good glassware or home furnishing stores. The finer the crystal, the greater the martini experience. Never use plastic! And you should also keep some crystal highball glasses handy for those who would drink their martinis on the rocks.

You will need a good stainless steel cocktail shaker. Stainless steel will chill a drink quickly and uniformly. For those who prefer their martini stirred, not shaken, a good mixing glass and a long stirring spoon are essential. Cocktail shakers and mixing glasses come in many designs and sizes. Anything from deco to modern or post-modern can be found if you look hard enough. Choose a shaker and mixing glass that complement your glassware. If you're ever stuck without a cocktail shaker, a tennis ball canister will do in a pinch.

There are several gadgets available to the martini mixer; they really aren't necessary, but they are fun. Eye droppers and misters for vermouth assure the very driest martini, and there's even something called a "martini tester" which allegedly checks the vermouth content of a martini.

There is much to explore beyond gin and vermouth. The modern martini mixer makes use of the flavored vodkas. Everything from coffee-flavored to pepper-flavored is on the shelves of your liquor store. You should include as many of them as possible when creating your martini bar. If you don't find a flavored vodka you need, you can always make your own. (The best pepper vodka is homemade.) Simply take the flavoring you desire—a hot pepper, a vanilla bean—and soak it in a bottle of plain vodka for at least a week. Taste it. If the vodka needs more flavor, soak it with the flavoring for a few more days. When the vodka is flavored the way you want it, strain it into a clean bottle.

Some distillers also make flavored gin, but this is not recommended—gin is flavorful enough on its own. A number of recipes in this book also call for scotch and rum, and any good home or office bar will include these other spirits on its shelves. Remember, quality counts. Be sure to buy the finest.

Also keep a good supply of cocktail olives on hand. Experiment with stuffed olives. They are delicious and can embolden many a martini. An almond-stuffed olive, a

15

jalapeño-stuffed olive, or a blue cheese-stuffed olive can change the character of a martini dramatically.

Garnishes for contemporary martinis go far beyond olives. Lemons, limes, and oranges should be part of your bar pantry, as well as cocktail onions. You will also have call for gumdrops, smoked oysters and clams, fresh berries in season, and pickled vegetables like asparagus and baby tomatoes. Read the recipes and see what you need. Explore the shelves of a gourmet store. There is no limit to what you can use as garnish. If you think it's a garnish, then it is.

Tools for making a martini are pretty basic. All you really need is a sharp paring knife for making citrus peel and zest. Citrus zesters are a nice labor saver and can be found in any kitchen store. Toothpicks are essential for creating elaborate garnishes.

Since temperature (cold!) is as important to a martini as gin, vodka, and vermouth are, all liquid ingredients should be stored in the freezer. They will not freeze. All garnishes also should be well-chilled in the refrigerator. An under-the-bar refrigerator/freezer is perfect for this purpose.

Finally, don't forget that the quality of the water used to make ice greatly affects the quality of a cocktail. Even if you are shaking and straining a drink, the ice should be made of pure spring or distilled water. Keep plenty on hand to make your ice.

SHAKERS

Decorative cocktail shakers and barware are stylish and useful additions to any martini bar. Ever since the birth of the cocktail, professional and home bartenders have used cocktail shakers not only to make drinks, but to make fashion statements. They add a touch of class.

Shakers have always reflected the design sensibilities of the era in which they're used. In many design museums you can find gorgeous Art Deco shakers from the 20s and 30s. These accoutrements served as conversation pieces as well as being utilitarian.

During the Great Depression of the 1930s, elegant bar-

ware was an affordable luxury for a "have-not" era. These gorgeous utensils not only made bartending an art, they deflected from the dingy realities of the 30s. Perhaps one could not travel to Paris, but one could recreate the elegant atmosphere of the Ritz with the right shaker and glass. And one could call to mind the elegance of a black tie evening with a novelty penguin cocktail shaker.

After World War II and into the 50s, as we entered the atomic age, barware began to look like rocket ships. Cocktail shakers were decorated with pictures of the atom and shaped like missiles.

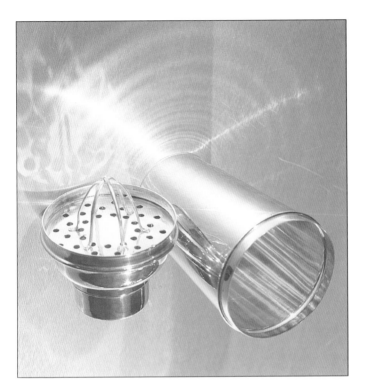

Early shakers were made of glass, silver plate, silver, Bakelite, and chromium. Glass is too fragile to be truly functional, but any metal shaker will do the job. Since the 1960s, most shakers have been made of stainless steel—a durable material that is excellent for completely chilling the cocktail.

Brand new shakers are available at houseware and department stores. High-end barware sets can be found at places like Tiffany's and Gump's. But if you're going to set up a martini bar in your home or office, we highly recommend a little antique hunting at flea markets and thrift shops. Almost every family before the late 70s had a full working bar at home, and the second-hand shops are full of these discarded treasures. Look for older, atomic-age silver shakers, or even older deco barware. You can start a collection for very little money, and have some usable art to display as you shake up martinis for your friends.

Martini—
The Drink of Presidents
and Publicists

Since its invention,
the martini has been the preferred cocktail
of presidents and heads-of-state.
FDR even carried a martini "kit"
on international summits, and Gerald Ford
thought the martini the exemplar of civilized life.
Prize-winning writers have sung its praise,
allowing themselves one (E.B. White)
or several (William Faulkner) for fortification
when facing the empty page.

Certainly not the sole territory of powerful men,
Dorothy Parker enjoyed martinis as did (and do)
many women journalists and authors.
As the three martini lunch comes back into favor,
look for the well-manicured and metallic-polished fingers
of book publicists and fashion editors
to be lifting their cocktail glasses at the Four Seasons,
a publishing haven,
whilst they toast the new millenium.

22

Famous Martini Drinkers

Robert Benchley

Humphrey Bogart

Luis Buñuel

Herb Caen

Raymond Chandler

Winston Churchill

William Faulkner

F. Scott and Zelda Fitzgerald

Gerald Ford

Robert Frost

Jackie Gleason

Ernest Hemingway

John F. Kennedy

Dorothy Lewis (Sinclair Lewis' wife)

H. L. Mencken

Dorothy Parker

Franklin Delano Roosevelt

E. B. White

Billy Wilder

P. G. Wodehouse

Alexander Woollcott

MARTINI RECIPES

25

Absolute Martini

5 parts vodka
1 part triple sec
2 parts fresh lemon juice
1 dash orange bitters

Combine all ingredients in a cocktail shaker with cracked ice and shake well. Strain into a chilled cocktail glass.

Allen Cocktail

4 parts gin
1 part maraschino liqueur
1/2 teaspoon fresh lemon juice
Lemon twist

Combine liquid ingredients in a cocktail shaker with cracked ice and shake well. Strain into a chilled cocktail glass and garnish with lemon twist.

Allen Cocktail

Ernest Hemingway was a correspondent
during World War II and covered the
liberation of Paris. He also personally saw to the
"liberation" of the Ritz in the Place Vendome.
After the Allies had liberated the city, Hemingway and
a group of journalist friends went to the Ritz.
The hotel was not damaged, but it was empty except
for the manager, who welcomed them
and put them into rooms.
When asked what they needed,
Hemingway ordered fifty martinis.

Allies Cocktail

3 parts gin
2 parts dry vermouth
1 teaspoon Jagermeister

Combine all ingredients in a cocktail shaker with cracked
ice and stir. Strain into a chilled cocktail glass.

Alternatini

6 parts vodka
1/2 teaspoon sweet vermouth
1/2 teaspoon dry vermouth
1 teaspoon white crème de cacao
Sweetened cocoa powder
Hershey's® kiss

Rim a chilled cocktail glass with sweetened cocoa powder.
Combine liquid ingredients in a cocktail shaker with
cracked ice and shake well. Strain into cocktail glass and
garnish with Hershey's® kiss.

Aperitivo

6 parts gin
3 parts white Sambuca
3 to 5 dashes orange bitters
Orange peel

Combine liquid ingredients in a mixing glass with ice cubes and stir. Strain into a chilled cocktail glass and garnish with orange peel.

Apple Pie Martini

6 parts vanilla flavored vodka
1 part Calvados
1 part dry vermouth
Apple slice

Combine liquid ingredients in a cocktail shaker with cracked ice and shake well. Strain into a chilled cocktail glass and garnish with a thin slice of apple.

Armada Martini

6 parts vodka
2 parts amontillado sherry
Orange twist

Combine liquid ingredients in a mixing glass with cracked ice and stir. Strain into a chilled cocktail glass and garnish with orange twist.

Artillery Cocktail

6 parts gin
2 parts sweet vermouth

Combine ingredients in a cocktail shaker with cracked ice and shake well. Strain into a chilled cocktail glass.

Babyface Martini

6 parts strawberry-flavored vodka
1 part dry vermouth
1/2 teaspoon maraschino liqueur
Fresh strawberry

Combine liquid ingredients in a cocktail shaker with cracked ice and shake well. Strain into a chilled cocktail glass and garnish with strawberry.

Barbed Wire

6 parts vodka
1 teaspoon sweet vermouth
1/2 teaspoon Pernod
1/2 teaspoon Chambord
Lemon twist

Combine liquid ingredients in a cocktail shaker with cracked ice and shake well. Strain into a chilled cocktail glass and garnish with lemon twist.

Barnum

6 parts gin
1 part apricot brandy
3 to 5 dashes Angostura bitters
3 to 5 dashes lemon juice

Combine all ingredients in a cocktail shaker with cracked ice and shake well. Strain into a chilled cocktail glass.

Beadlestone

6 parts Scotch
3 parts dry vermouth

Combine ingredients in a mixing glass with ice cubes and stir well. Strain into a chilled cocktail glass.

Bennett

6 parts gin
1/2 teaspoon bar sugar
3 to 5 dashes Angostura bitters

Combine all ingredients in a cocktail shaker with cracked ice and shake well. Strain into a chilled cocktail glass.

Berrytini

6 parts currant vodka
1 part raspberry eau-de-vie
Fresh raspberries

Combine vodka and eau-de-vie in a cocktail shaker with cracked ice and shake well. Strain into a chilled cocktail glass and garnish with raspberries.

Black & White Martini

6 parts vanilla vodka
2 parts crème de cacao
Black & white licorice candies

Combine liquid ingredients in a cocktail shaker with cracked ice and shake well. Strain into a chilled cocktail glass and garnish with black & white licorice candies.

Black & White
Martini

"After four martinis,
my husband turns into
a disgusting beast.
And after the fifth,
I pass out altogether."

ANONYMOUS

Black Dog

6 parts light rum
1 part dry vermouth
Pitted black olive

Combine liquid ingredients in mixing glass with cracked ice and stir well. Strain into a chilled cocktail glass and garnish with olive.

Bloodhound

Bloodhound

6 parts gin
2 parts sweet vermouth
2 parts dry vermouth

3 fresh strawberries, hulled
Fresh strawberries for garnish

Combine all ingredients in a blender and mix until well-blended. Pour into a chilled cocktail glass and garnish with fresh strawberry.

Blue Moon Martini

6 parts gin
1 part blue curaçao
Lemon twist

Combine liquid ingredients in a mixing glass with ice cubes and stir well. Strain into a chilled cocktail glass and garnish with lemon twist.

Blue Moon
Martini

Blue-on-Blue Martini

6 parts vodka
1 part blue curaçao

1 dash Angostura bitters
Cocktail olive

Combine liquid ingredients in a cocktail shaker with cracked ice and shake well. Strain into a chilled cocktail glass and garnish with olive.

Boardwalk

6 parts vodka
2 parts dry vermouth
1/2 teaspoon maraschino liqueur
1 teaspoon fresh lemon juice
Lemon twist

Combine liquid ingredients in a
cocktail shaker with cracked ice
and shake well. Strain into a
chilled cocktail glass and garnish
with lemon twist.

Boomerang Martini

6 parts gin
1 dash Angostura bitters
2 parts dry vermouth
1 dash maraschino liqueur
Kiwi slice

Stir all liquid ingredients with ice
cubes in a mixing glass. Strain into
a chilled cocktail glass and garnish
with kiwi slice.

Broadway Martini

6 parts gin
1 part white crème de menthe
Fresh mint sprig

Combine liquid ingredients in a
cocktail shaker with cracked ice
and shake well. Strain into a
chilled cocktail glass and garnish
with mint sprig.

Boomerang Martini

The search—
some might say obsession—
for the driest martini continues.
One company sells
vermouth atomizers. Another sells
olives marinated in vermouth.
The driest martini is straight gin,
but even those have been
sent back to the bartender for
not being dry enough.

Bronx Terrace Cocktail

6 parts gin
2 parts fresh lime juice
1 part dry vermouth
Maraschino cherry

Combine liquid ingredients in a cocktail shaker with cracked ice and shake well. Strain into a chilled cocktail glass and garnish with cherry.

Brown Cocktail

4 parts gin
2 parts light rum
1 part dry vermouth
Kumquat

Stir all ingredients in a mixing glass with cracked ice. Strain into a chilled cocktail glass and garnish with kumquat.

Brown Cocktail

In the 1940s, John Lardner reported that the New York Yankees ball club had hired private detectives to keep track of their players. He noted that they "should have been easy to stalk because, belonging to a high-class ball club, they drank martinis and left a trail of olives."

Buckeye Martini

6 parts gin
1 part dry vermouth
Black olive

Combine liquid ingredients in a cocktail shaker with cracked ice and shake well. Strain into a chilled cocktail glass and garnish with black olive.

Cabaret Martini

6 parts gin
3 parts Dubonnet rouge
3 to 5 dashes Angostura bitters
3 to 5 dashes Pernod
Lime twist

Combine liquid ingredients in a cocktail shaker with cracked ice and shake well. Strain into a chilled cocktail glass and garnish with lime twist.

California Martini

6 parts vodka
1 part red wine
1 tablespoon dark rum
3 to 5 dashes orange bitters
Orange twist

Combine liquid ingredients in a cocktail shaker with cracked ice and shake well. Strain into a chilled cocktail glass and garnish with orange twist.

Cajun Martini

6 parts pepper vodka
1 dash of dry vermouth
Olive stuffed with pickled jalapeño pepper

Combine liquid ingredients in a mixing glass with cracked ice and stir. Strain into a chilled cocktail glass and garnish with olive.

Hot night on the Bayou. While others sipped their Sazeracs, Remy mixed me a Cajun Martini. When I bit into that vermouth-soaked olive stuffed with the jalapeño, a chill ran up and down my spine and my eyes opened wide. "Mmmm, good, honey! Now that's a martini!"

Campari Martini

6 parts vodka
1 part Campari
Lime twist

Combine liquid
ingredients in a
cocktail shaker
with cracked ice and
shake well. Strain
into a chilled
cocktail glass and
garnish with lime
twist.

She'd spent two months in Italy, touring and
looking for hidden Renaissance frescoes.
One evening in Florence, just after sunset, she
wandered into an American bar and ordered a
martini. The bartender winked at her and said,
"Cara, let me make you a martini `a la Italiano,"
and he served her a Campari Martini. To this day,
when she wants to remember Tuscany, no matter
where she is, all she needs to do is
make herself this Florentine specialty.

Caribou Martini

4 parts coffee-flavored vodka, chilled
Champagne or dry sparkling wine
Lemon twist
Coffee bean

Pour chilled vodka into a cocktail glass. Top off with champagne and stir gently. Garnish with lemon twist and drop in a coffee bean.

Caribou
Martini

A TRUE STORY: They were both fans of the television show "Northern Exposure". And the more they corresponded, the more they discovered how much they had in common—a love for science fiction, an appreciation of fine champagne and gourmet coffee, lacy underthings (he, to look; she, to wear), and, of course, martinis. Their first date was a seven-hour phone call. When they finally met in person, they were in love. They celebrated their first anniversary with the creation of the Caribou Martini.

Chocolate Martini

6 parts vodka
1 part chocolate liqueur
Chocolate curl

Combine vodka and liqueur in a mixing glass with ice cubes and stir. Strain into a chilled cocktail glass and garnish with chocolate curl.

Some families have eggnog recipes that have been passed down through generations. Others have a favorite wassail they share. No family is more sophisticated when it comes to Yuletide than the Fosters, who have celebrated Christmas since before Prohibition with their special Christmas Martini.

Christmas Martini

6 parts gin
1 part dry vermouth
1 teaspoon peppermint schnapps
Miniature candy cane

Combine liquid ingredients in a cocktail shaker with cracked ice and shake well. Strain into a chilled cocktail glass and garnish with candy cane.

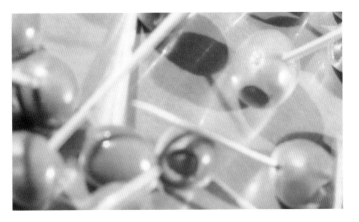

Christmas Tini

6 parts vodka
1 teaspoon peppermint schnapps
1 part dry vermouth
Miniature candy cane

Combine liquid ingredients in a cocktail shaker with cracked ice and shake well. Strain into a chilled cocktail glass and garnish with candy cane.

Winston Churchill
was a martini aficionado.
Here is his recipe for a martini.
It is not unlike that of most fans of
the extremely dry martini.
Some people whisper,
"vermouth."
Others,
like Churchill,
look at the bottle.

Churchill's Martini

6 parts gin
Bottle of dry vermouth
Cocktail olive

Shake gin in a cocktail shaker with cracked ice. Strain into a chilled cocktail glass and look at the bottle of vermouth. Garnish glass with olive.

Church
Lady Martini

4 parts gin
2 parts dry vermouth
2 parts fresh orange juice
Lemon, lime, and orange wedges

Combine liquid ingredients in a cocktail shaker with cracked ice and shake well. Strain into a chilled cocktail glass. Garnish with fruit wedges.

Church
Lady
Martini

Citrus Martini

8 parts lemon-flavored vodka
1 teaspoon Grand Marnier or orange liqueur
1 teaspoon fresh lime juice
Lemon twist

Combine liquid ingredients in a cocktail shaker
with cracked ice and shake well. Strain into a
chilled cocktail glass and garnish with lemon
twist.

Coffee Lover's Martini

6 parts coffee-flavored vodka
1 part dry vermouth
1 part Frangelico
Coffee beans

Combine liquid ingredients in a cocktail shaker with
cracked ice and shake well. Strain into a chilled cocktail
glass and garnish with a few coffee beans.

Skip the hot toddies!
There's a martini
to suit any occasion—
even the flu.

Cold Comfort Martini

4 parts lemon vodka
4 parts honey vodka
Lemon twist

Combine vodkas in a cocktail
shaker with cracked ice and shake
well. Strain into a chilled cocktail
glass and garnish with lemon
twist.

Colony Club Martini

6 parts gin
1 teaspoon Pernod
3 to 5 dashes orange bitters
Orange twist

Combine liquid ingredients in a cocktail shaker with cracked ice and shake well. Strain into a chilled cocktail glass and garnish with orange twist.

Cosmopolitan

4 parts vodka
2 parts triple sec
2 parts cranberry juice
1 part fresh lime juice

Combine ingredients in a cocktail shaker with cracked ice and shake well. Strain into a chilled cocktail glass.

Crantini

6 parts gin
1 part unsweetened cranberry juice
Lime or lemon twist

Pour gin into a chilled cocktail glass. Slowly add the cranberry juice. Garnish with lime or lemon twist.

Crantini

"Got a light?" He looked up
to see a beautiful woman holding an unlit Arturo
Fuente in her delicate fingers. "You shouldn't smoke.
It's bad for you," he said. "How about a drink?"
She paused, and put the cigar in her purse. She
smiled. "Better make it something healthy, buddy—
to rid my body of all this nasty, delicious, cigar smoke."
"But of course."

He ordered her a Crantini.

Crimson Martini

6 parts gin
1 part ruby port
2 teaspoons fresh lime juice
1 teaspoon grenadine
Lime twist

Combine liquid ingredients in a cocktail shaker with cracked ice and shake well. Strain into a chilled cocktail glass and garnish with lime twist.

Almost a daiquiri,
but not quite.
We like to think that Papa
drank these in Havana,
but Hemingway was a stickler
when it came to his martinis.
This drink might have
passed muster with him,
but he would never have
called it a martini.

Cuban Martini

6 parts light rum
1 part dry vermouth
Granulated sugar
Lime twist

Rim a chilled cocktail glass with
sugar. Combine liquid ingredients
in a cocktail shaker with cracked ice
and shake well. Strain into cocktail
glass and garnish with lime twist.

Danish Martini

6 parts aquavit
1 part dry vermouth
Cocktail olive

Combine liquid ingredients in a
cocktail shaker with cracked ice
and shake well. Strain into a chilled
cocktail glass and garnish with
olive.

Daydream Martini

6 parts citrus vodka
1 part triple sec
2 parts fresh orange juice
1/4 teaspoon bar sugar

Combine all ingredients in a mixing glass with cracked ice and stir well. Strain into a chilled cocktail glass.

Deep Sea Martini

6 parts gin
2 parts dry vermouth
1/2 teaspoon Pernod
1 dash orange bitters

Combine all ingredients in a mixing glass with cracked ice and stir well. Strain into a chilled cocktail glass.

Delicious Martini

6 parts coffee-flavored vodka
1 part Grand Marnier
Orange twist

Combine liquid ingredients in a cocktail shaker with cracked ice and shake well. Strain into a chilled cocktail glass and garnish with orange twist.

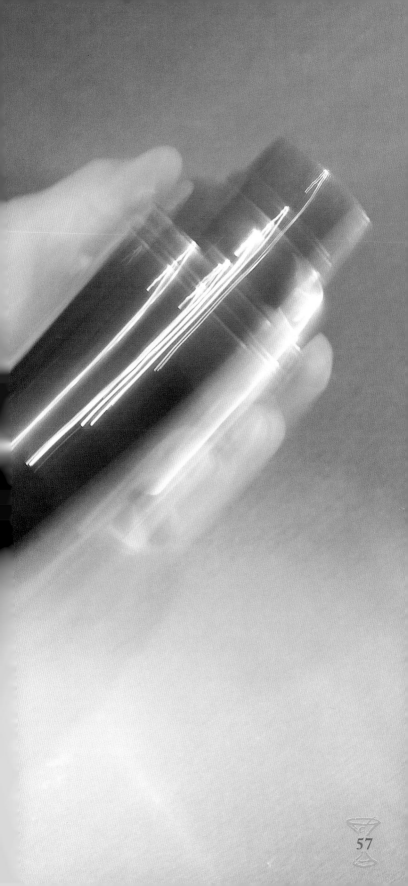

Desperate Martini

6 parts gin
1 part dry vermouth
1 part blackberry brandy
Fresh blackberries (optional)

Combine liquid ingredients in a cocktail shaker with cracked ice and shake well. Strain into a chilled cocktail glass and garnish with fresh blackberries.

It is said that
Jackie Gleason once ordered a martini
at a bar in a fashionable Miami Beach hotel.
When the bartender asked him
if he wanted a twist of lemon with it,
he exclaimed,
"When I want a goddam lemonade,
I'll ask for it!"

Dirty Martini

6 parts gin
2 parts dry vermouth
1 part olive brine
Cocktail olives

Combine liquid ingredients in a cocktail shaker with cracked ice and shake well. Strain into a chilled cocktail glass and garnish with one or two olives.

E. B. White
had a more conservative approach
to his favorite cocktail than most writers.
"Before I start to write,
I always treat myself to a nice dry martini.
Just one, to give me the courage
to get started.
After that, I am on my own."

Dirty Martini

Dirty Vodka Martini

6 parts vodka
2 parts dry vermouth

1 part olive brine
Cocktail olives

Combine liquid ingredients in a cocktail shaker with cracked ice and shake well. Strain into a chilled cocktail glass and garnish with one or two olives.

Double Fudge Martini

6 parts vodka
Chocolate cocktail straw

1 part chocolate liqueur
1 part coffee liqueur

Combine liquid ingredients in a mixing glass with cracked ice and stir well. Strain into a chilled cocktail glass and garnish with chocolate straw.

East Wing

6 parts vodka
1 part Campari

2 parts cherry brandy
Lemon twist

Combine liquid ingredients in a cocktail shaker with cracked ice and shake well. Strain into a chilled cocktail glass and garnish with lemon twist.

Eat My Martini

6 parts honey vodka
1 part amontillado sherry
Almond-stuffed olive

Combine liquid ingredients in a cocktail shaker with cracked ice and shake well. Strain into a chilled cocktail glass and garnish with olive.

Emerald Martini

The martini is enjoying a renaissance during this last decade of the millennium, but gin is not. Two out of three martinis ordered at bars are made with vodka.

Emerald Martini

6 parts citrus-flavored vodka
2 parts chartreuse

Lemon twist
Lime twist

Combine liquid ingredients in a mixing glass with cracked ice and stir well. Strain into a chilled cocktail glass and garnish with lemon and lime twists.

Nick and Nora Charles,
the sophisticated sleuthing couple from
The Thin Man novels and movies,
were dyed-in-the-wool martini drinkers.
Nick used to measure out the vermouth
with an eye dropper.

Extra Dry Vodka Martini

4 parts vodka   **1/8 teaspoon lemon juice**
3 to 5 drops dry vermouth   **Lemon twist**

Combine liquid ingredients in a cocktail shaker with
cracked ice and shake well. Strain into a chilled cocktail
glass and garnish with lemon twist.

W. H. Auden often prepared for his lectures
with a few martinis. On one occasion in 1947,
he had a few too many before he spoke at Harvard.
The topic was supposed to have been
Miguel de Cervantes, but when Auden stood up
at the podium, he apologized for his new dentures,
and then told the eager crowd that he'd never been able
to read Don Quixote to the end, and
bet that no one in the audience had either.

Fare Thee Well Martini

6 parts gin
1 part dry vermouth
1 dash sweet vermouth
1 dash Cointreau

Combine all ingredients in a mixing glass with cracked ice
and stir well. Strain into a chilled cocktail glass.

63

Farmer's Martini

6 parts gin
1 part dry vermouth

1 part sweet vermouth
3 to 5 dashes Angostura bitters

Combine all ingredients in a cocktail shaker with cracked ice and shake well. Strain into a chilled cocktail glass.

FDR WAS A SERIOUS MARTINI DRINKER
AND CARRIED A MARTINI "KIT" WITH HIM
WHENEVER HE TRAVELED.
DURING THE TEHERAN CONFERENCE,
HE INSISTED ON MIXING ONE OF HIS SPECIALTIES
FOR JOSEPH STALIN. STALIN FOUND IT
"COLD ON THE STOMACH," BUT LIKED IT.
FDR'S MARTINI WAS MOST LIKELY
THE FIRST "DIRTY MARTINI."

FDR's Martini

2 parts gin
1 part vermouth

1 teaspoon olive brine
Lemon twist
Cocktail olive

Rub the lemon twist around the rim of a chilled cocktail glass and discard the peel. Combine gin, vermouth, and olive brine in a cocktail shaker with cracked ice and shake well. Strain into chilled glass and garnish with olive.

Fifty-Fifty Martini

4 parts gin
4 parts dry vermouth
Cocktail olive

Combine liquid ingredients in a mixing glass with cracked ice and stir well. Strain into a chilled cocktail glass and garnish with olive.

The martini reached
the height of popularity in the 1950s.
One Manhattan bar served martinis
"dry, extra dry, or very dry."
The drier the martini,
the more the drink cost.

Fifty-Fifty Vodka Martini

4 parts vodka
4 parts dry vermouth
Cocktail olive

Combine liquid ingredients in a mixing glass with cracked ice and stir well. Strain into a chilled cocktail glass and garnish with olive.

"I've got to get out of these wet clothes
and into a dry martini."
This immortal line has been attributed
to Robert Benchley, Billy Wilder, and
Alexander Woollcott. No one is sure who
actually said it. All three men were known for their
bon mots. My money's on Woollcott, drama critic for
the New York Times during the 1920s and 1930s.
He also appeared in several screwball comedies.
It is believed he uttered this line after shooting
a scene where he was tossed into a
swimming pool, fully clothed.

Fine and Dandy

4 parts gin
2 parts triple sec

2 parts fresh lemon juice
1 dash orange bitters

Combine all ingredients in a cocktail shaker with cracked ice and shake well. Strain into a chilled cocktail glass.

The martini seems to lend itself to more jokes
and apocryphal stories than all other cocktails.
One of the more famous stories goes like this:
A man arrives at a restaurant several minutes
before his wife to instruct the head waiter,
"No matter what kind of soup I order,
fill the tureen with martinis.
My wife has a fit if I order even one drink."
His instructions were followed out,
and then the man called to the waiter:
"I'll have some more soup,
and this time, make it extra-dry."

Fino Martini

6 parts gin or vodka
1 teaspoon fino sherry
Lemon twist

Combine liquid ingredients in a mixing glass with ice
cubes and stir well. Strain into a chilled cocktail glass and
garnish with lemon twist.

Fretful Martini

6 parts gin
1 part blue curaçao

1 dash Angostura bitters
Cocktail olive

Combine liquid ingredients in a cocktail shaker with
cracked ice and shake well. Strain into a chilled cocktail
glass and garnish with olive.

Frozen Martini

5 parts gin
1 part dry vermouth
2 almond-stuffed cocktail olives

Place gin, vermouth, olives, cocktail glass, and cocktail
shaker in freezer for at least 3 hours. When all compo-
nents are thoroughly chilled, combine gin and vermouth
in the chilled cocktail shaker and shake well. Place the two
frozen olives in the chilled cocktail glass and pour the gin
and vermouth mixture over it.

Fuzzy Martini

4 parts vanilla-flavored vodka
1 part coffee-flavored vodka
1 teaspoon peach schnapps
Fresh peach slice

Combine liquid ingredients in a cocktail glass and garnish
with a fresh peach slice.

The Gibson is thought to be named
for the famed Gibson Girls, Charles Dana Gibson's
lovely pinups of the early twentieth century.
The two cocktail onions are believed
to represent breasts.

Gibson

8 parts gin or vodka
3 to 5 dashes dry vermouth
2 cocktail onions

Combine liquid
ingredients in a mixing
glass with ice cubes
and stir well.
Strain into a chilled
cocktail glass and
garnish with onions.

The last shot
of the day on a movie
set is called the
"Martini Shot".

Gilroy Martini

6 parts buffalo grass vodka
2 parts dry vermouth
2 drops garlic juice
Garlic-stuffed olive

Combine liquid ingredients
in a cocktail shaker with cracked
ice and shake well. Strain into a
chilled cocktail glass and
garnish with olive.

Gimlet

8 parts gin or vodka
2 parts Rose's lime juice

Combine all ingredients in a
cocktail shaker with cracked ice
and shake well. Strain into a
chilled cocktail glass.

Gin and It

8 parts gin
2 parts sweet vermouth
Lemon twist

Combine liquid ingredients in a
cocktail shaker with cracked ice
and shake well. Strain into a
chilled cocktail glass and garnish
with lemon twist.

William Faulkner loved the
strong drink that eventually killed him.
In the years before he was completely
incapacitated by alcohol, he couldn't write
without having a few martinis beforehand.
He wrote, "When I have one martini,
I feel bigger, wiser, taller.
When I have a second, I feel superlative.
When I have more,
there's no holding me."

Gimlet

Golf Martini

The martini is a thoroughly modern cocktail.
Even though the drink was most likely
invented in the nineteenth century, it did
not gain popularity until well into the twentieth.
After Prohibition, the martini gained in popularity.
After World War II, martinis got drier,
and sweeter drinks lost their appeal.
By the mid-1950s, the true mark of a sophisticate
was a dry, icy gin martini, with only a trace of
vermouth. Here's a variation on the classic.

Golf Martini

8 parts gin
3 to 5 dashes Angostura bitters

2 parts dry vermouth
Cocktail olive

Combine liquid ingredients in a mixing glass with cracked ice and shake well. Strain into a chilled cocktail glass and garnish with olive.

Great Caesar's Martini

6 parts vodka
1 part dry vermouth
Anchovy-stuffed olive

Combine liquid ingredients in a cocktail shaker with cracked ice and shake well. Strain into a chilled cocktail glass and garnish with olive.

Green Martini

6 parts gin
1 part chartreuse
Almond-stuffed olive

Combine liquid ingredients in a cocktail shaker with cracked ice and shake well. Strain into a chilled cocktail glass and garnish with olive.

Gumdrop Martini

4 parts lemon-flavored rum
2 parts vodka
1 part Southern Comfort
1/2 teaspoon Dry vermouth

1 part fresh lemon juice
Bar sugar
Lemon slice
Gumdrops

Rim a chilled cocktail glass with bar sugar. Combine liquid ingredients in a cocktail shaker with cracked ice and shake well. Strain into the chilled cocktail glass and garnish with lemon slice and gumdrops.

How Much Vermouth?

The original recipe
for the dry martini
actually wasn't very dry
by today's standards.
The proportions were
two parts gin to
one part French or
dry vermouth.

Gypsy Martini

8 parts gin
2 parts sweet vermouth
Maraschino cherry

Combine liquid ingredients in a cocktail shaker with cracked ice and shake well. Strain into a chilled cocktail glass and garnish with cherry.

Hasty Martini

6 parts gin
1 part dry vermouth
3 to 5 dashes Pernod
1 teaspoon grenadine

Combine all ingredients in a cocktail shaker with cracked ice and shake well. Strain into a chilled cocktail glass.

Hep Cat

6 parts berry vodka
1 part dry vermouth
1 dash sweet vermouth
1 dash Cointreau

Combine all ingredients in a mixing glass with cracked ice and stir well. Strain into a chilled cocktail glass.

Hoffman House Martini

8 parts gin   **3 to 5 dashes orange bitters**
1 part dry vermouth **Cocktail olive**

Combine liquid ingredients in a mixing glass with cracked ice and stir well. Strain into a chilled cocktail glass and garnish with olive.

William Randolph Hearst used to entertain Hollywood stars at his San Simeon estate in Cambria, California. But "W. R." was a teetotaler. Upon arrival, each guest's luggage was searched for offending bottles and flasks. Gin was confiscated and only returned to the guest when he or she left. Fortunately for the Hollywood crowd, Hearst's staff was not above being bribed, and a well-placed gratuity allowed gin to flow at San Simeon, albeit in secret.

Hollywood Martini

6 parts gin
1 part Goldwasser
1 part dry vermouth
1 blue cheese-stuffed olive

Combine liquid ingredients in a cocktail shaker with cracked ice and shake well. Strain into a chilled cocktail glass and garnish with olive.

Homestead Martini

6 parts gin
2 parts sweet vermouth
Orange twist

Combine liquid ingredients in a mixing glass with ice and stir well. Strain into a chilled cocktail glass and garnish with orange twist.

Homestead
Martini

Honeydew Martini

6 parts vodka
1 part Midori

1 part triple sec
Lemon twist

Combine liquid ingredients in a cocktail shaker with cracked ice and shake well. Strain into a chilled cocktail glass and garnish with lemon twist.

Hoosier Cocktail

4 parts buffalo grass vodka
2 parts light rum
1 part dry vermouth

Combine all ingredients in a mixing glass with cracked ice and stir well. Strain into a chilled cocktail glass.

Hot & Dirty Martini

6 parts pepper vodka
1 part dry vermouth
1 teaspoon olive brine
Olive stuffed with pickled jalapeño pepper

Combine liquid ingredients in a cocktail shaker with cracked ice and shake well. Strain into a chilled cocktail glass and garnish with olive.

Hotel Plaza Cocktail

2 parts gin
2 parts dry vermouth

2 parts sweet vermouth
Maraschino cherry

Combine liquid ingredients in a mixing glass with ice cubes and stir well. Strain into a chilled cocktail glass and garnish with cherry.

In the never-ending quest for the coldest and the driest martini, one has to make this inevitable choice: Straight up or on the rocks? Each has its advantages and drawbacks. Ideally, all liquid ingredients should be stored in the freezer, and glasses should be chilled, thus making ice superfluous. But there is much to be said for the bell-like tones of ice cubes tinkling in a crystal highball glass. Are you willing to risk diluting your martini with melting ice? Or are you a purist, the thought of a martini on the rocks simply not part of your world? This variation will work either way.

Ideal Martini

6 parts gin
2 parts dry vermouth

1/2 teaspoon maraschino liqueur
1 teaspoon fresh lemon juice
Lemon twist

Combine liquid ingredients in a cocktail shaker with cracked ice and shake well. Strain into a chilled cocktail glass and garnish with lemon twist.

Imperial Martini

6 parts gin
2 parts dry vermouth

1/2 teaspoon maraschino liqueur
3 to 5 dashes Angostura bitters

Combine all ingredients in a mixing glass with ice and stir well. Strain into a chilled cocktail glass.

"In and out"
refers to the method of mixing this martini.

In and Out Martini

7 parts vodka
Dry vermouth

2 blue cheese-stuffed olives
Lemon twist

Pour vermouth into a well-chilled martini glass. Swish it around and then discard. Pour vodka into the glass and garnish with olives and lemon twist.

Irish Martini

6 parts buffalo grass vodka
1 part dry vermouth
Irish whiskey
Lemon twist

Rinse a chilled cocktail glass with Irish whiskey. Combine vodka and vermouth in a cocktail shaker with cracked ice and shake well. Strain into cocktail glass and garnish with lemon twist.

Imperial Martini

83

85

In Havana, Ernest Hemingway
had a many-martini lunch
with famous prizefighter Gene Tunney.
As the two men got drunker, Hemingway got
belligerent and tried to goad Tunney into a fight.
(Hemingway considered himself quite
the authority on boxing.) He kept punching at Tunney.
Tunney, ever the gentleman, asked Hemingway to stop.
But he would not. Finally, Tunney decided
to give him a little "liver punch,"
just to get him to stop,
and he let him have it. Hemingway buckled,
his face went gray, and Tunney thought he was
going to go out. But he didn't, and after that,
Hemingway was the perfect gentleman
for the rest of the afternoon.

Island Martini

6 parts gold rum
1 part dry vermouth
1 part sweet vermouth
Lemon twist

Combine liquid ingredients in a cocktail shaker with
cracked ice and shake well. Strain into a chilled cocktail
glass and garnish with lemon twist.

Jack London Martini

6 parts currant vodka
2 parts Dubonnet blanc
1 part maraschino liqueur
Lemon twist

Combine liquid ingredients in a cocktail shaker with
cracked ice and shake well. Strain into a chilled cocktail
glass and garnish with lemon twist.

Jamaican Martini

6 parts gin
1 part red wine
1 tablespoon dark rum
3 to 5 dashes orange bitters
Cherry peppers

Combine liquid ingredients in a cocktail shaker with cracked ice and shake well. Strain into a chilled cocktail glass and garnish with cherry peppers.

James Bond Martini

6 parts gin
2 parts vodka
1 part Lillet blanc
Lemon twist

Combine liquid
ingredients in a
cocktail shaker with
cracked ice and shake
well. Strain into a
chilled cocktail glass
and garnish with
lemon twist.

Jamie's Martini

6 parts vodka
1 part triple sec
2 parts fresh orange juice
1/4 teaspoon bar sugar

Combine all ingredients in a mixing glass with cracked ice and stir well. Strain into a chilled cocktail glass.

H. L. Mencken usually drank beer,
but made an exception when he spent
an evening with Philip Goodman.
When Mencken came up to New York from Baltimore,
he and Goodman would go to a speakeasy
in Union City, New Jersey, and
eat a dinner of knockwurst, boiled beef, sauerkraut,
mashed potatoes, and cheesecake.
They would wash this down with
several beers and coffees.
They would then return to Manhattan,
stop at a restaurant on West Forty-Fourth Street,
have more cheesecake and some strudel,
and more coffee and more beer.
They would always end the evening
by having double martinis.
Goodman believed that the gin aided digestion—
that it "oxidized" the food.

Journalist Martini

6 parts gin
1 teaspoon dry vermouth
1 teaspoon sweet vermouth
1 teaspoon triple sec
1 teaspoon fresh lime juice
1 dash Angostura bitters

Combine all ingredients in a cocktail shaker with cracked ice and shake well. Strain into a chilled cocktail glass.

One of the many martini legends credits the bartender at the Knickerbocker Hotel, a Manhattan hotel popular at the turn of the century, as the martini's creator.

Knickerbocker

6 parts gin
2 parts dry vermouth
1/2 teaspoon sweet vermouth
Lemon twist

Combine liquid ingredients in a mixing glass with cracked ice and stir well. Strain into a chilled cocktail glass and garnish with lemon twist.

Kup's Indispensable Martini

6 parts gin
1 1/2 parts dry vermouth
1 1/2 parts sweet vermouth
Orange twist

Combine liquid ingredients in a cocktail shaker with cracked ice and shake well. Strain into a chilled cocktail glass and garnish with orange twist.

Kyoto

6 parts gin
2 parts melon liqueur
Melon ball

1 part dry vermouth
1/4 teaspoon fresh lemon juice

Combine liquid ingredients in a mixing glass with ice cubes and stir well. Strain into a chilled cocktail glass and garnish with melon ball.

Leap Year Martini

6 parts citrus-flavored vodka
1 part sweet vermouth
1 part Grand Marnier
1/2 teaspoon fresh lemon juice

Combine all ingredients in a cocktail shaker with cracked ice and shake well. Strain into a chilled cocktail glass.

Sylvia Plath, Anne Sexton, and George Starbuck
all took Robert Lowell's creative writing course
at the Boston Center for Adult Education.
After each class, they would pile into
Sexton's old Ford, drive to the Ritz Hotel,
and park illegally in a loading zone—
Sexton explaining,
"It's OK, we're only going to get loaded."
They then proceeded into the Ritz to have
three or four martinis each.

Lemon Drop Martini

6 parts lemon-flavored vodka
1 part dry vermouth

Granulated sugar
Lemon twist

Rim a chilled cocktail glass with granulated sugar.
Combine liquid ingredients in a cocktail shaker with
cracked ice and shake well. Strain into cocktail glass
and garnish with lemon twist.

Another martini joke:
A slightly tipsy guest at a party approaches
the host and asks, "Do lemons have legs?"
"Lemons with legs!
You must be completely gone!," replies the host.
"Oh dear," sighs the guest,
"I'm afraid I've just squeezed your canary
into my martini."

Lemon Twist

6 parts lemon-flavored rum
1 part dry vermouth
Lemon twist

Combine liquid ingredients in a cocktail shaker with
cracked ice and shake well. Strain into a chilled cocktail
glass and garnish with lemon twist.

London Martini

6 parts gin
1/2 teaspoon maraschino liqueur
3 to 5 dashes orange bitters
1/2 teaspoon bar sugar
Lemon twist

Combine liquid ingredients in a mixing glass and stir well. Pour mixture into a cocktail shaker with cracked ice and shake well. Strain into a chilled cocktail glass and garnish with lemon twist.

James Bond's vodka martini—
"shaken not stirred"—
was a radical concept when Ian Fleming
introduced it as a "Vesper" in Casino Royale. A martini
was never shaken, and it had to be made with gin.
But who would argue with James Bond? His
"Vesper" started a martini revolution. Today, much
to purists' chagrin, vodka martinis are more popular
than the original gin cocktail.

Low Tide Martini

6 parts vodka
1 part dry vermouth
Lime twist

1 teaspoon clam juice
Olive stuffed with smoked clam

Combine liquid ingredients in a cocktail shaker with
cracked ice and shake well. Strain into a chilled cocktail
glass and garnish with olive and lime twist.

Macaroon

6 parts vodka
1 part chocolate liqueur
1 part Amarretto
Orange twist

Combine liquid ingredients in a mixing glass with cracked
ice and stir well. Strain into a chilled cocktail glass and
garnish with orange twist.

Mama's Martini

6 parts vanilla vodka
1 part apricot brandy
3 to 5 dashes Angostura bitters
3 to 5 dashes lemon juice

Combine all ingredients in a cocktail shaker with cracked
ice and shake well. Strain into a chilled cocktail glass.

Manhasset

6 parts rye whiskey
1/2 part dry vermouth
1/2 part sweet vermouth
1 tablespoon fresh lemon juice
Lemon twist

Combine liquid ingredients in a cocktail shaker with cracked ice and shake well. Strain into a chilled cocktail glass and garnish with lemon twist.

Manhasset

A Manhattan is thought to be the "opposite" of a martini. While a martini is made with clear liquor, gin or vodka, and dry vermouth, a Manhattan is made with amber whiskey and sweet vermouth (and don't forget the bitters)!

Is a cherry really the opposite of an olive?

Manhattan

6 parts rye whiskey
2 parts sweet vermouth

1 dash Angostura bitters
Maraschino cherry

Combine liquid ingredients in a mixing glass with ice and stir well. Strain into a chilled cocktail glass and garnish with cherry.

Maritime Martini

6 parts gin
2 parts dry vermouth
Anchovy-stuffed olive

Combine liquid ingredients in a cocktail shaker with cracked ice and shake well. Strain into a chilled cocktail glass and garnish with olive.

Some say the martini was developed in Europe, others in New York. But I believe that this elegant drink had its not so elegant beginnings in the 1860s, in California, after the Gold Rush. Apparently, the martini was invented by a man about to hop on the ferry from Martinez, California, to San Francisco. He needed some fortification for the journey across the Bay. All there was at hand was some rot-gut gin. To take the burn off the gin, he mixed it with an equal part of vermouth, and sweetened it with a few drops of maraschino and orange bitters. And the martini, or "Martinez Cocktail," was born— a California native.

Martinez Cocktail

4 parts gin
2 parts sweet vermouth
1 part maraschino liqueur

1 teaspoon sugar syrup (optional)
1-3 dashes Angostura bitters

Combine all ingredients in a mixing glass with cracked ice and stir well. Strain into a chilled old-fashioned glass.

100

It was our first date.
I was nervous, I was shy.
I was 22 years old, and I'd never
been to Peacock Alley.
Was I overdressed? Underdressed?
Could he see that my manicure
wasn't perfect?
Was I wearing too much Opium?
We met for cocktails.
We sat on a couch near
Cole Porter's piano. The sounds
of Gershwin filled the air—
my favorite song,
"Embraceable You"—and my
knees felt weak. The waiter came to
take our order. I stammered.
He ordered for me,
"A Bombay Martini, straight up,"
and smiled. I was a virgin.
This was new.
But I sipped the icy drink
and felt warm.
After that evening,
he showed me much more,
but I'll always remember
my first martini.

Martini

6 parts gin
1 part dry vermouth
Cocktail olive

Combine liquid ingredients in a
mixing glass with ice cubes and stir
well. Strain into a chilled cocktail
glass and garnish with olive.

Martini Milano

4 parts gin
1 part dry vermouth
1 part dry white wine
1 teaspoon Campari
Lime twist

Combine liquid ingredients in a cocktail shaker with cracked ice and shake well. Strain into a chilled cocktail glass and garnish with lime twist.

Martini Navratilova

6 parts vodka
2 parts dry vermouth
3 to 5 dashes orange bitters

Combine all ingredients in a cocktail shaker with cracked ice and shake well. Strain into a chilled cocktail glass.

Martinis for Four

1 cup gin
1 tablespoon dry vermouth
4 large pimento-stuffed green olives

Fill a 4-cup glass measuring cup 1/3 full with ice. Add gin and vermouth and stir gently. Immediately strain mixture into chilled martini glasses. Add an olive to each glass and serve immediately.

Martunia

6 parts gin   **1 part sweet vermouth**
1 part dry vermouth **Edible flowers**

Combine liquid ingredients in a cocktail shaker with cracked ice and shake well. Strain into a chilled cocktail glass and garnish with edible flower petals.

The Ritz bar in Paris was and is a favorite haunt of many literary figures. James Jones and William Styron once spent all night getting drunk and continued into the next day. They ended up at the Ritz at noon, drinking straight-up martinis. At about three in the afternoon, they decided to call it a night.

Metropolitan

6 parts currant vodka
1 part Lillet blanc
1/2 teaspoon fresh lime juice
Lemon twist

Combine liquid ingredients in a cocktail shaker with cracked ice and shake well. Strain into a chilled cocktail glass and garnish with lemon twist.

Mocha Blanca Martini

6 parts coffee-flavored vodka
2 parts white chocolate liqueur
White chocolate curl

Combine liquid ingredients in a mixing glass and stir well. Strain into a chilled cocktail glass and garnish with chocolate curl.

Moll Flanders

4 parts gin
2 parts sloe gin
2 parts dry vermouth
3 to 5 dashes Angostura bitters

Combine all ingredients in a mixing glass with cracked ice and stir well. Strain into a chilled cocktail glass.

John Lardner posits
that the drinks of primitive people
are apt to be sweet and thick.
The martini, then, represents the most advanced
and sophisticated civilization,
since it is clear, cold, thin, and dry.
This is the ultimate martini—
the "Naked" Martini—
the zenith of a civilized people.

Naked Martini

6 parts gin
Cocktail olive

Chill gin in freezer for at least 2 hours. Pour gin into a chilled cocktail glass and garnish with olive.

Luis Buñuel, the great film director,
had his own recipe for a very dry martini:
"Connoisseurs who like their martinis very dry
suggest simply allowing a ray of sunlight
to shine through the bottle of Noilly Prat
before it hits the gin."

Negroni

4 parts gin
2 parts Campari
1 part sweet vermouth
Orange twist

Combine liquid ingredients in a cocktail shaker with
cracked ice and shake well. Strain into a chilled cocktail
glass and garnish with orange twist.

Newbury

6 parts gin
2 parts sweet vermouth
1 part triple sec
Lemon twist

Combine liquid ingredients in a cocktail shaker with
cracked ice and shake well. Strain into a chilled cocktail
glass and garnish with lemon twist.

New Orleans Martini

6 parts vanilla vodka
1 parts dry vermouth
1 part Pernod
1 dash Angostura bitters
Fresh mint sprig

Combine liquid ingredients in a cocktail shaker with
cracked ice and shake well. Strain into a chilled cocktail
glass and garnish with mint sprig.

Negroni

Nightmare

6 parts gin
2 parts Madeira wine
2 parts cherry brandy
Orange twist

Combine liquid ingredients in a mixing glass with cracked ice and stir well. Strain into a chilled cocktail glass and garnish with orange twist.

Ninotchka

6 parts vanilla-flavored vodka
2 parts white chocolate liqueur
1 part fresh lemon juice

Combine all ingredients in a cocktail shaker with cracked ice and shake well. Strain into a chilled cocktail glass.

Northern Exposure Moose Martini

6 parts currant-flavored vodka
1 teaspoon Chambord liqueur
Juniper berries soaked in vermouth

Combine liquid ingredients in a cocktail shaker with cracked ice and shake well. Strain into a chilled cocktail glass and garnish with juniper berries.

In the early 1940s,
a martini at Pete's Tavern
would run you fifty cents. This may explain
why so many starving writers and artists
made it their home away from home.
The more successful ones were drinking
at the Algonquin.

Nutty Martini

6 parts vodka
1 part Frangelico
Lemon twist

Combine liquid ingredients in a cocktail shaker with cracked ice and shake well. Strain into a chilled cocktail glass and garnish with lemon twist.

Oakland Cocktail

4 parts vodka
2 parts dry vermouth
2 parts fresh orange juice

Combine all ingredients in a cocktail shaker with cracked ice and shake well. Strain into a chilled cocktail glass.

Octopus's Garden

6 parts gin
2 parts dry vermouth
Smoked baby octopus
Black olive

Combine liquid ingredients in a cocktail shaker with cracked ice and shake well. Strain into a chilled cocktail glass and garnish with olive and octopus.

My grandmother swore
this recipe came straight from the old country
and that it was my duty to pass it on.

Old Country Martini

6 parts vodka
2 parts Madeira wine
2 parts cherry brandy
Orange twist

Combine liquid ingredients in a mixing glass with cracked ice and stir well. Strain into a chilled cocktail glass and garnish with orange twist.

The writers of the
famed Algonquin Roundtable
loved their martinis.
But when they gathered in the Rose Room,
Prohibition was law,
and the Algonquin Hotel was legally dry.
To alleviate this problem,
after a meal, the denizens of the Roundtable
would visit their friend, Neysa McMein,
who lived in the hotel.
She had a still in her bathroom.

Opal Martini

6 parts gin
1 part triple sec
2 parts fresh orange juice
1/4 teaspoon bar sugar

Combine all ingredients
in a mixing glass with
cracked ice and shake
well. Strain into a
chilled cocktail glass.

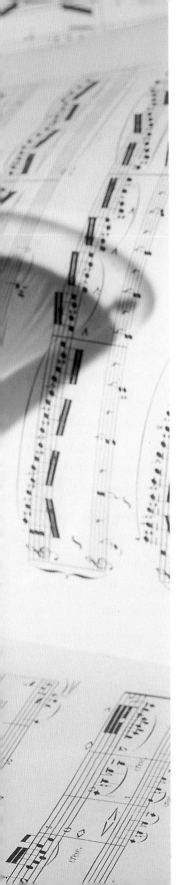

When Oscar Wilde
toured the United States
on a lecture tour
in the 1880s,
he impressed Leadville,
Colorado miners
with his ability to
out-drink them.
Their drink of choice?
Gin, with dry vermouth.

Opera Martini

6 parts gin
2 parts Dubonnet blanc
1 part maraschino liqueur
Lemon twist

Combine liquid ingredients
in a cocktail shaker with
cracked ice and shake
well. Strain into a chilled
cocktail glass and garnish
with lemon twist.

Orange Martini

6 parts vodka
1 part triple sec
1 dash orange bitters
Orange twist

Combine liquid ingredients in a
cocktail shaker with cracked ice
and shake well. Strain into a chilled
cocktail glass and garnish with
orange twist.

Osaka Dry

6 parts vodka
1 part sake
Pickled plum

Combine liquid ingredients in a
cocktail shaker with cracked ice
and shake well. Strain into a chilled
cocktail glass and garnish with
plum.

Oyster Martini

6 parts vodka
1 part dry vermouth
Smoked oyster

Combine liquid ingredients in a
cocktail shaker with cracked ice
and shake well. Strain into a chilled
cocktail glass and garnish with a
smoked oyster on a toothpick.

Paisley Martini

6 parts gin
1/2 teaspoon dry vermouth
1/2 teaspoon Scotch
Cocktail olive

Combine liquid ingredients
in a cocktail shaker with
cracked ice and shake well.
Strain into a chilled
cocktail glass and
garnish with olive.

Pall Mall Martini

4 parts gin
1 part dry vermouth
1 part sweet vermouth
1 teaspoon white crème de menthe
1 dash orange bitters

Combine all ingredients in a mixing glass with ice cubes and stir well. Strain into a chilled cocktail glass.

Palm Beach Martini

6 parts gin
1 teaspoon sweet vermouth
4 parts grapefruit juice

Combine all ingredients in a cocktail shaker with cracked ice and shake well. Strain into a chilled cocktail glass.

Parrothead Martini

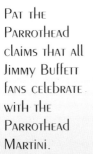

Pat the Parrothead claims that all Jimmy Buffett fans celebrate with the Parrothead Martini.

6 parts silver tequila
1 part triple sec
1 teaspoon fresh lime juice
Lime twist

Combine liquid ingredients in a cocktail shaker with cracked ice and shake well. Strain into a chilled cocktail glass and garnish with lime twist.

Parisian Martini

6 parts gin
2 parts dry vermouth
1 part crème de cassis

Combine all ingredients in a cocktail shaker with cracked ice and shake well. Strain into a chilled cocktail glass.

"New York is
the greatest city in the world for lunch,"
said William Emerson, Jr.
"And when that first martini hits the liver
like a silver bullet,
there is a sigh of contentment
that can be heard in Dubuque."

Park Avenue Martini

6 parts gin
1 part sweet vermouth
1 part pineapple juice

Combine all ingredients in a cocktail shaker with cracked ice and shake well. Strain into a chilled cocktail glass.

Peach Blossom Martini

6 parts peach vodka
1 part Dubonnet rouge
1 part maraschino liqueur
Fresh peach slice

Combine liquid ingredients in a cocktail shaker with cracked ice and shake well. Strain into a chilled cocktail glass and garnish with peach slice.

Peppermint
Martini

Peachy Martini

6 parts strawberry-flavored vodka
2 parts peach brandy
Lemon twist

Combine liquid ingredients in a cocktail shaker with cracked ice and shake well. Strain into a chilled cocktail glass and garnish with lemon twist.

Peggy's Martini

6 parts gin
1 part sweet vermouth
1/2 teaspoon Dubonnet rouge
1/2 teaspoon Pernod

Combine all ingredients in a mixing glass with cracked ice and stir well. Strain into a chilled cocktail glass.

Peppermint Martini

6 parts pepper vodka
2 parts white crème de menthe
Fresh mint sprig

Combine liquid ingredients in a cocktail shaker with cracked ice and shake well. Strain into a chilled cocktail glass and garnish with mint sprig.

Here's another classic cocktail joke.
A visitor to a midtown bar orders a Manhattan.
When it's placed before him, he notices that there's a
sprig of parsley floating on top.
"What is that THING in my Manhattan?"
he asks the bartender. The bartender replies,
without blinking,
"That, sir, is Central Park."

Perfect Manhattan

6 parts rye whiskey
1 part dry vermouth
1 part sweet vermouth
Maraschino cherry

Combine liquid ingredients in a cocktail shaker with
cracked ice and shake well. Strain into a chilled cocktail
glass and garnish with cherry.

The first martini?
Anecdotal history tells us
that in 1608
Henry Hudson served gin
to the Lenape Indians
on an unnamed island.
The Lenapes became very drunk,
and when they recovered,
named the island "Manhachtanienk" or
"the island where we became intoxicated."
Over the years, this name evolved into
"Manhattan."

Perfect Martini

6 parts gin
1 part dry vermouth
1 part sweet vermouth
Cocktail olive

Combine liquid ingredients in a cocktail shaker with
cracked ice and shake well. Strain into chilled cocktail
glass and garnish with olive.

Picadilly Martini

6 parts gin
2 parts dry vermouth
1/2 teaspoon Pernod
1 dash grenadine

Combine all ingredients in a mixing glass with ice and stir well. Strain into a chilled cocktail glass.

If you order a martini in England,
you'll probably be served a glass of sweet vermouth.
Be on the safe side,
and order the British version of the martini—
"Pink Gin."

Pink Gin Martini

8 parts gin
1 teaspoon Angostura bitters

Pour bitters into a cocktail glass and swirl around until the inside of the glass is completely coated with the bitters. Pour gin into the glass. This drink should be served at room temperature.

Plaza Martini

2 parts gin
2 parts dry vermouth
2 parts sweet vermouth

Combine all ingredients in a cocktail shaker with cracked ice and shake well. Strain into a chilled cocktail glass.

Pompano Martini

5 parts gin   **2 parts fresh grapefruit juice**
1 part dry vermouth   **1 dash orange bitters**

Combine all ingredients in a cocktail shaker with cracked ice and shake well. Strain into a chilled cocktail glass.

Pretty Martini

4 parts vodka   **1 part Amaretto**
1 part Grand Marnier   **1 part dry vermouth**
Orange twist

Combine liquid ingredients in a cocktail shaker with cracked ice and shake well. Strain into a chilled cocktail glass and garnish with orange twist.

Prince Edward Martini

6 parts gin
1 part Drambuie
Lemon twist

Combine liquid ingredients in a cocktail shaker with cracked ice and shake well. Strain into a chilled cocktail glass and garnish with lemon twist.

Princess Elizabeth Martini

6 parts sweet vermouth
1 part dry vermouth
2 teaspoons Benedictine

Combine all ingredients in a cocktail shaker with cracked ice and shake well. Strain into a chilled cocktail glass.

Quarterdeck Martini

6 parts berry vodka
1 part maraschino liqueur
1 part grapefruit juice
Fresh mint sprig

Combine liquid ingredients in a mixing glass with cracked ice and stir well. Strain into a chilled cocktail glass and garnish with mint sprig.

Queen Elizabeth Martini

6 parts gin
1 part dry vermouth
2 teaspoon Benedictine

Combine all ingredients in a cocktail shaker with cracked ice and shake well. Strain into a chilled cocktail glass.

Racquet Club

6 parts gin
2 parts dry vermouth
3 to 5 dashes orange bitters

Combine all ingredients in a cocktail shaker with cracked ice and shake well. Strain into a chilled cocktail glass.

Red Dog Martini

6 parts vodka
1 part ruby port
2 teaspoons fresh lime juice
1 teaspoon grenadine
Lime twist

Combine liquid ingredients in a cocktail shaker with cracked ice and shake well. Strain into a chilled cocktail glass and garnish with lime twist.

Renaissance Martini

6 parts gin
1 part fino sherry
Grated nutmeg

Combine liquid ingredients in a cocktail shaker with
cracked ice and shake well. Strain into a chilled cocktail
glass and garnish with nutmeg.

Rendezvous

6 parts gin
2 parts cherry brandy
1 part Campari
Fresh cherries

Combine liquid ingredients in a cocktail
shaker with cracked ice and shake well.
Strain into a chilled cocktail glass and
garnish with fresh cherry.

Although most agree
that the martini was invented in the 1860s
in Northern California,
the drink did not achieve
widespread recognition in the United States
until after Prohibition.
It might have become more popular earlier,
but the Volstead Act put an end to its ascension.
During Prohibition, gin was the easiest
of the hard liquors to bootleg, and rot-gut—
bathtub gin—became ubiquitous.
It's no coincidence that sweet mixed drinks
also became prevalent then.
Drinkers wanted to mask the taste
of the harsh homemade stuff.
When Prohibition ended, people could at last get fine,
imported gin, and there was no need to dilute it.
The martini, once again,
was on its way to immortality.

Resolution Martini

6 parts gin
2 parts apricot brandy
1 part fresh lemon juice

Combine ingredients in a cocktail shaker with cracked ice
and shake well. Strain into a chilled cocktail glass.

Road Runner Martini

6 parts pepper vodka   **1 part gold tequila**
1 part dry vermouth   **Jalapeño stuffed olive**

Combine liquid ingredients in a cocktail shaker with
cracked ice and shake well. Strain into a chilled cocktail
glass and garnish with olive.

Rum Martini

Rolls Royce

6 parts gin
2 parts dry vermouth
2 parts sweet vermouth
1/4 teaspoon Benedictine

Combine ingredients in a cocktail shaker with cracked ice and shake well. Strain into a chilled cocktail glass.

Rum Martini

6 parts light rum
1 part dry vermouth
1 dash orange bitters
Almond-stuffed olive

Combine liquid ingredients in a cocktail shaker with cracked ice and shake well. Strain into a chilled cocktail glass and garnish with olive.

Russian Martini

4 parts vodka
4 parts gin
1 part white chocolate liqueur

Combine liquid ingredients in a cocktail shaker with cracked ice and shake well. Strain into a chilled cocktail glass.

Russian Rose

6 parts strawberry-flavored vodka
1 part dry vermouth
1 part grenadine
1 dash orange bitters

Combine all ingredients in a mixing glass with cracked ice and stir well. Strain into a chilled cocktail glass.

Saketini

6 parts gin
1 part sake
Lemon twist wrapped with
Pickled ginger

Combine liquid ingredients in a cocktail shaker with cracked ice and shake well. Strain into a chilled cocktail glass and garnish with lemon twist.

Secret Martini

6 parts gin
2 parts Lillet blanc
2 dashes Angostura bitters
Cocktail olive

Combine liquid ingredients in a mixing glass with cracked ice and stir well. Strain into a chilled cocktail glass and garnish with olive.

Saketini

Seventh Heaven

6 parts gin
1 part maraschino liqueur
1 part grapefruit juice
Fresh mint sprig

Combine liquid ingredients in a mixing glass with cracked ice and stir well. Strain into a chilled cocktail glass and garnish with mint sprig.

Sexy Devil

4 parts vodka
2 parts cranberry vodka
1 part dry vermouth
Fresh strawberry
Lemon peel

Combine liquid ingredients in a cocktail shaker with cracked ice and shake well. Strain into a chilled cocktail glass and garnish with lemon peel and strawberry.

Shrimptini

6 parts gin or vodka
2 parts dry vermouth
Dash of Tabasco®
Large cooked shrimp

Combine liquid ingredients in a cocktail shaker with cracked ice and shake well. Strain into a chilled cocktail glass and garnish with and cooked shrimp.

Silver Streak

"Silver bullet"
is one the martini's nickname.
Sleek and elegant, powerful and cold,
a Silver Bullet always hits its mark.
The Silver Streak is another variation
on a theme.

Silver Streak

6 parts gin
3 parts Jagermeister
Lemon twist

Combine liquid ingredients in a mixing glass with cracked ice and stir well. Strain into a chilled cocktail glass and garnish with lemon twist.

Sloe Gin Martini

6 parts sloe gin
2 parts dry vermouth
3 to 5 dashes Angostura bitters
Lemon twist

Combine liquid ingredients in a cocktail shaker with cracked ice and shake well. Strain into a chilled cocktail glass and garnish with lemon twist.

Smoky Martini

6 parts gin
1 part dry vermouth
1 teaspoon scotch
Lemon twist

Combine liquid ingredients in a mixing glass with cracked ice and stir well. Strain into a chilled cocktail glass and garnish with lemon twist.

Southern Martini

6 parts gin
1 part triple sec
3 to 5 dashes orange bitters
Lemon twist

Combine liquid ingredients in a mixing glass with cracked ice and stir well. Strain into a chilled cocktail glass and garnish with lemon twist.

The relationship
between a Russian and a bottle of vodka
is almost mystical.

—Richard Owen

Soviet Martini

6 parts ashberry-flavored or currant vodka
1 part dry vermouth
1 part fino sherry
Lemon twist

Combine liquid ingredients in a mixing glass with cracked ice and stir well. Strain into a chilled cocktail glass and garnish with lemon twist.

Spiced Treat Martini

6 parts cinnamon vodka
1 part chocolate liqueur
1 part coffee liqueur
Chocolate cocktail straw

Combine liquid ingredients in a mixing glass with cracked ice and stir well. Strain into a chilled cocktail glass and garnish with chocolate straw.

Springtime Martini

6 parts buffalo grass vodka
2 parts Lillet blanc
Miniature pickled asparagus spear

Combine liquid ingredients in a cocktail shaker with cracked ice and shake well. Strain into a chilled cocktail glass and garnish with asparagus spear.

Staten Island Cocktail

6 parts coffee vodka
1 part dry vermouth
2 parts fresh lime juice
Maraschino cherry

Combine liquid ingredients in a cocktail
shaker with cracked ice and shake well.
Strain into a chilled cocktail glass and
garnish with cherry.

Sweet and Spicy Martini

6 parts cinnamon vodka
1 part sweet vermouth
1 part orange liqueur
Cinnamon stick

Combine liquid ingredients in a cocktail
shaker with cracked ice and shake well.
Strain into a chilled cocktail glass and
garnish with cinnamon stick.

In one musical number
of the 1949 Broadway production of
"Gentlemen Prefer Blondes,"
Miles White's award-winning costumes
featured two martinis per showgirl—
one over each breast—
with nipples doing double duty
as olives.

Strawberry Blonde

6 parts strawberry vodka
2 parts Lillet blanc
Fresh strawberry

Combine liquid ingredients in a cocktail shaker with
cracked ice and shake well. Strain into a chilled cocktail
glass and garnish with fresh strawberry.

St.Petersburg

6 parts vodka
3 to 5 dashes orange bitters
Orange peel

Combine liquid ingredients in a cocktail
shaker with cracked ice and shake well.
Strain into a chilled cocktail glass and
garnish with orange peel.

Summer Breeze

6 parts citrus vodka
2 parts melon liqueur
1 part dry vermouth
1/4 teaspoon fresh lemon juice
Melon ball

Combine liquid ingredients in a mixing glass with ice cubes and stir well. Strain into a chilled cocktail glass and garnish with melon ball.

Sweet Martini

6 parts gin
2 parts sweet vermouth
1 dash orange bitters
Orange twist

Combine liquid ingredients in a mixing glass with cracked ice and stir well. Strain into a chilled cocktail glass and garnish with orange twist.

Sweetie Martini

6 parts gin
1 part dry vermouth
1 part sweet vermouth
Lemon twist

Combine liquid ingredients in a cocktail shaker with cracked ice and shake well. Strain into a chilled cocktail glass and garnish with lemon twist.

"The three-martini lunch
is the epitome of American efficiency.
Where else can
you get an earful, a bellyful, and a snootful
at the same time?"
—Gerald Ford

Tequini

6 parts silver tequila
1 part dry vermouth
1 dash orange bitters
Lemon twist

Combine liquid ingredients in a cocktail shaker with
cracked ice and shake well. Strain into a chilled cocktail
glass and garnish with lemon twist. Note: Enhance this
drink by rubbing the lemon twist over the rim of the glass.

Raymond Chandler,
the great American mystery novelist,
really didn't want to write the screenplay
for the film of "The Blue Dahlia," so he struck a deal
with his producer, John Houseman.
He agreed to write the script only
if it was written into his contract that he could
write it while drunk. The contract
also had to include the following:
Paramount would provide limousines, secretaries,
and nurses for Chandler 24 hours a day,
a doctor would be on call to administer vitamin shots
since Chandler never ate when he was drinking,
and there would be a direct phone line
from his house to the studio.
The studio would also take the Chandlers' maid shopping.
Houseman agreed to this over lunch with Chandler,
at which time Chandler had three double martinis
and three stingers.
He went straight to work after lunch
and finished the screenplay
in about two weeks.

Third Degree Martini

6 parts gin
2 parts dry vermouth
1 part Pernod
Star anise

Combine liquid ingredients in a cocktail shaker with cracked ice and shake well. Strain into a chilled cocktail glass and garnish with star anise.

Three Stripes

4 parts gin
2 parts dry vermouth
2 parts fresh orange juice

Combine all ingredients in a cocktail shaker with cracked ice and shake well. Strain into a chilled cocktail glass.

Tootsie Roll Martini

6 parts vodka
1 part chocolate liqueur
1 part Grand Marnier
Orange twist

Combine liquid ingredients in a cocktail shaker with cracked ice and shake well. Strain into a chilled cocktail glass and garnish with orange twist.

Tovarisch

6 parts vodka
2 parts kümmel
2 parts fresh lime juice
Black olive

Combine liquid ingredients in a cocktail shaker with cracked ice and shake well. Strain into a chilled cocktail glass and garnish with black olive.

Tovarisch

Truffle Martini

6 parts strawberry vodka **1 part chocolate liqueur**
1 part Grand Marnier **Orange twist**

Combine liquid ingredients in a cocktail shaker with
cracked ice and shake well. Strain into a chilled cocktail
glass and garnish with orange twist.

Turf Martini

4 parts gin
2 parts dry vermouth
1 part Pernod
1 part fresh lemon juice
3 to 5 dashes Angostura bitters
Almond-stuffed olive

Combine liquid ingredients in a cocktail shaker with
cracked ice and shake well. Strain into a chilled cocktail
glass and garnish with olive.

Tuxedo

4 parts vodka
3 parts dry vermouth
1/2 teaspoon maraschino liqueur
3 to 5 dashes orange bitters
Lemon twist

Combine liquid ingredients in a cocktail shaker with
cracked ice and shake well. Strain into a chilled cocktail
glass and garnish with lemon twist.

Ulanda

4 parts gin
2 parts triple sec
1 tablespoon Pernod

Combine all ingredients in a mixing glass with cracked ice
and stir well. Strain into a chilled cocktail glass.

Valencia
Martini

Valencia Martini

6 parts gin
2 parts amontillado sherry
Olive

Combine liquid ingredients in a mixing glass with cracked ice and stir well. Strain into a chilled cocktail glass and garnish with olive.

Vanilla Twist

6 parts vanilla vodka
1 part Cointreau
1 part dry vermouth
Vanilla bean

Combine liquid ingredients in a cocktail shaker with cracked ice and shake well. Strain into a chilled cocktail glass and garnish with vanilla bean.

Ian Fleming's James Bond
not only drank vodka martinis,
he also drank champagne, sherry, scotch—
whatever the occasion called for.
But the cinematic James Bond was a hard-core
vodka martini drinker, largely because Smirnoff bought
the product placement rights.
The popularity of the movies helped make the vodka martini
the most popular drink of the 60s.
Today, two out of three martinis
are made with vodka.

Vodka Martini

6 parts vodka
2 parts dry vermouth (or to taste)
Olive

Combine liquid ingredients in a cocktail shaker with cracked ice and shake well. Strain into a chilled cocktail glass and garnish with olive.

Vanilla Twist

6 parts pineapple vodka
1 part dry vermouth
1 part Lillet blanc
Pineapple wedge

Combine liquid ingredients in a cocktail shaker
with cracked ice and shake well. Strain into a chilled
cocktail glass and garnish with pineapple wedge.

Warsaw Martini

4 parts potato vodka
1 part dry vermouth
1 part blackberry brandy
1 tablespoon fresh lemon juice

Combine all ingredients in a cocktail shaker with cracked ice and shake well. Strain into a chilled cocktail glass.

Wembly Martini

6 parts gin
1 part dry vermouth
1 teaspoon apricot brandy
1 teaspoon Calvados
Lemon twist

Combine liquid ingredients in a cocktail shaker with cracked ice and shake well. Strain into a chilled cocktail glass and garnish with lemon twist.

What Is That Martini?

6 parts vodka
1 part Sambuca
Licorice twist
3 coffee beans

Combine liquid ingredients in a mixing glass with cracked ice and stir well. Strain into a chilled cocktail glass and garnish with licorice twist and coffee beans.

Woo Woo Martini

6 parts cranberry vodka
1 part peach schnapps
Lemon twist

Combine liquid ingredients in a cocktail shaker with
cracked ice and shake well. Strain into a chilled cocktail
glass and garnish with lemon twist.

Xena Martini

5 parts honey-flavored vodka
1 part buffalo grass vodka
1 teaspoon Lillet blanc
Pickled asparagus spear

Combine liquid ingredients in a cocktail shaker with
cracked ice and shake well. Strain into a chilled cocktail
glass and garnish with asparagus spear.

Zippy Martini

6 parts vodka
1 part dry vermouth
3 to 4 dashes Tabasco® sauce
Pickled jalapeño pepper slice

Combine liquid ingredients in a cocktail shaker with
cracked ice and shake well. Strain into a chilled cocktail
glass and garnish with pepper.

Recipe Index

My Own Martini Recipes

Send us your martini recipes if they are not included in The Martini Book. We'd love to hear about them and with your permission use in future editions.
Send recipes to: Black Dog & Leventhal
                151 W. 19th Street
                New York, NY 10011

183

My Own
Martini Recipes

Send us your martini recipes if they are not included in <u>The</u> <u>Martini</u> <u>Book.</u> We'd love to hear about them and with your permission use in future editions.
Send recipes to: Black Dog & Leventhal
                    151 W. 19th Street
                    New York, NY 10011

185

My Own
Martini Recipes

Send us your martini recipes if they are not included in <u>The</u> <u>Martini</u> <u>Book.</u> We'd love to hear about them and with your permission use in future editions.
Send recipes to: Black Dog & Leventhal
                    151 W. 19th Street
                    New York, NY 10011

187